a. martin

Agnes Martin

—

On Beauty

Edited by Milly Glimcher

PACE

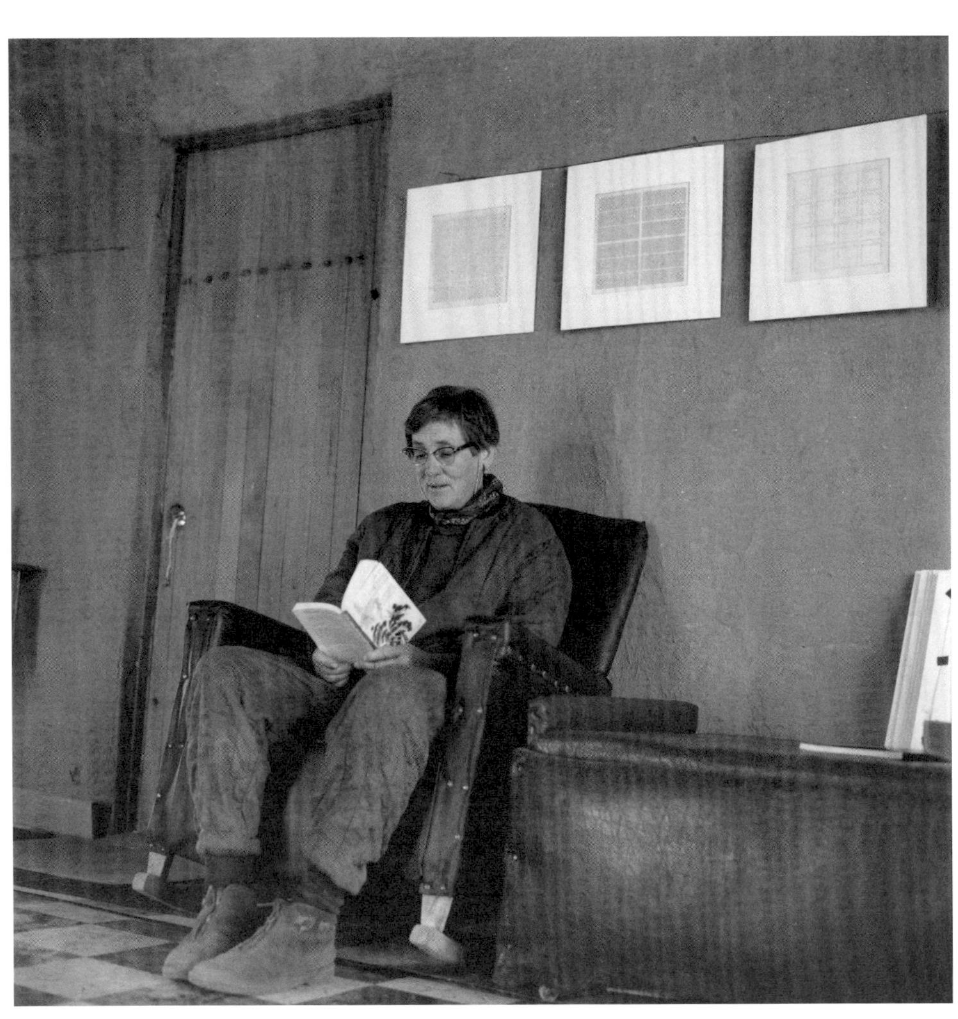

TABLE OF CONTENTS

The underside of the leaf

Cool in shadow

Sublimely unemphatic

Smiling of innocence

The frailest stems

Quivering in light

Bend and break

In silence

This poem, like the paintings, is not really about nature. It is not
what is seen. It is what is known forever in the mind.

In our minds there is an awareness of perfection

and when we look with our eyes we see it.

 Blessings 2000 acrylic and graphite on canvas 60 × 60"

The Current of the River of Life Moves Us

What we really want to do is serve happiness.

We want everyone to be happy, never unhappy even for a moment.
We want the animals to be happy. The happiness of every living
thing is what we want.

We want it very much but we cannot bring it about.

We cannot make even one individual happy.

It seems that this thing that we want most of all is out of our reach.

But we were born to serve happiness and we do serve it.

The confusion is due to our lack of awareness of real happiness.

Happiness is pervasive.

It is everywhere. And everywhere the same.

And it is forever.

When people are really happy they say: "This will last forever even
after death," and that is true.

When we are unhappy it is because something is covering our
minds and we are not able to be aware of happiness. When the
difficulty is past we find happiness again.

It is not that happiness is all around us. That is not it at all. It is not this or that or in this or that.

It is an abstract thing.

Happiness is unattached. Always the same. It does not appear and disappear. It is not sometimes more and sometimes less. It is our awareness of happiness that goes up and down.

Happiness is our real condition. It is reality. It is life. In this life, life is represented by beauty and happiness.

If you are completely unaware of them you are not alive.

The times when you are not aware of beauty and happiness you are not alive.

When we see life we call it beauty. It is magnificent — wonderful.

We may be looking at the ocean when we are aware of beauty but it is not the ocean. We may be in the desert and we say that we are aware of the "living desert" but it is not the desert.

Life is ever present in the desert and everywhere, forever.

By awareness of life we are inspired to live.

Life is consciousness of life itself.

The measure of your life is the amount of beauty and happiness of which you are aware.

The life of an artist is a very good opportunity for life.

When we realize that we can see life we gradually give up the things that stand in the way of our complete awareness.

As we paint we move along step by step. We realize that we are guided in our work by awareness of life.

We are guided to greater expression of awareness and devotion to life.

We recognize the great exultation with life of great artists like Beethoven and we realize that all great artists praise and exult life.

The life of an artist is completely unmaterialistic, because beauty and happiness and life are all the same and they are pervasive, unattached and abstract and they are our only concern.

They are immeasurable, completely lacking in substance. They are perfect and sublime.

This is the subject matter of art.

Naturally artists become passionately devoted to life — not to
material living, not to the conventional idea of life but to the life
that we see.

The fields speak and the hills speak "as though with tongues" and
what they say is wonderful.

You must say to yourself: "How can I best step into this state of
mind and devote myself to the expression of life."

You must not be led astray into the illustration of ideas because that
is not art work. It is ineffective even though it is often accepted
for a short time. It does not contribute to happiness and it is finally
discarded.

The art work in the Metropolitan Museum or the British Museum
does not illustrate ideas.

The great and fatal pitfall in the art field and in life is dependence
on the intellect rather than inspiration.

Dependence on intellect means a consideration of observed facts
and deductions from observation as a guide in life.

Dependence on inspiration means dependence on consciousness, a
growing consciousness that develops from awareness of beauty and
happiness.

To live and work by inspiration you have to stop thinking.

You have to hold your mind still in order to hear inspiration clearly.

Even now you can hear it saying "Yes" and "No." You look at a painting and say "Is this it," and your mind answers and says "Yes" or "No."

If it says "Yes" it means that you have just made the work that you should have made. What your mind says *never* applies to anyone else. This work is what is possible for you according to your awareness of life.

There are no criteria. No possibility for criticism.

By the use of intellect we have created a world of ideas that does not actually exist.

The political world is a structure conceived and agreed to by us but it is not a reality.

You have been conditioned to believe that this political world is in fact real.

With this conception it is believed that we have come into ownership of the world and that we are responsible for creating it. And with this concept we have placed ourselves in a condition of perpetual responsibility and reform.

But since we are not creating the world, since it was created before us and we are merely in it, and since we do not own it, our whole political concept is false.

It is untrue. It is not based in reality or true life.

An artist must see this and give up all reform and political considerations.

The world evolves due to changes that take place in individuals. By individuals I mean all living things.

The world evolves due to a growing awareness in the lives of all things and is expressed in their actions.

The actions of all things are guided by a growing awareness of life.

We call it inspiration.

Living by inspiration is living. Living by intellect — by comparisons, calculations, schemes, concepts, ideas — is all a structure of pride in which there is not beauty or happiness — no life.

The intellectual is in fact death.

I will give you an example: If you were at the beach and keenly aware of the shining waves, the fragrant air, the freedom of mind, feeling happy and free — that is reality. That is life. Now if someone

came on the beach with a radio and tuned it to the news — that is
the intellectual and political. You would feel the shock of moving
suddenly from reality to unreality. You would be depressed and
irritated.

The political is a negation of life. It is negative living, anti-life.
The divide and own concept. The we are the creators concept is
the concept of pride. Where pride walks, nothing of life remains.
It is the supreme destroyer of life. Pride leaves nothing in its path.
It is death in life.

All great visionaries agree that we move in this life from death to
life, from error to awareness of truth, from negation of life to total
awareness and devotion, passionate devotion to life from death to
everlasting life, from blindness to enlightenment, from uncon-
sciousness and dreams to consciousness.

I will describe to you the negative attitude toward life even though it
is ineffective and of no account. The negative person has no respect
for life, his own or anyone's. He is complaining and destructive and
convinced that to get ahead in life he must take advantage of others.
He is going to fight, born to fight — for his rights, for his ideas, in
self defense, and for his advantage.

All aggressiveness is negative regardless of the cause, except in the
defense of innocence. (In the defense of innocence we will all be
very brave. No practice is needed.)

We must not worry about the negative attitude in others. When I say the negative is of no account I mean it is ineffective negatively in life. Since it is part of life and life is positive, it is of course positive. And we can see dimly how the Mafia for instance preying on the weak makes them turn away from pride in themselves.

Evil in life is the actions that result from lack of respect for life.

That is enough for death, now for real life.

In real life we get everything we want and need, just like the grass. It is all laid on. *Fate is kind.* You will look back in old age and say: "I had everything I really wanted."

When we see someone who has been poor all his life we think that he has been deprived but in reality he was unable to want more than he had. His lack of potential for life limited his life. He lacked energy, zest, and gratitude.

Fate is kind. At every moment we are presented with happiness, the sublime, absolute perfection. We are unable to grasp it due to the pull of death, commonly known as weakness.

Fate is kind. In that beside the pull of death there is the pull of life, which is our desire to live fully and truly, a very strong pull indeed. When we engage in the battle with death the pull of life always wins. If death wins temporarily it means the battle is not over.

If you want life on your side or to be on the side of life against death you must surrender completely to life. You will have to make an about face because you have been conditioned to responsibility.

There are lots of parents who would like their children to be artists but when they get to this point of surrender to life they change their minds. Everyone who cannot himself surrender to life will be antagonistic.

It is in this way that an artist becomes a pariah. He is described as egocentric when in reality he sacrifices the most. The children of artists are very well off because their parents are guided by life, and life dictates that innocence must be protected *as the source*. The wives of artists also if they are more innocent than their husbands will be protected.

If you are on the side of life you are warned not to offend against innocence and if you disobey your own mind you are rendered helpless.

It is the same with painting. If the word from your mind is that the painting is not good enough and you decide to fight the world for it, you have rejected your inspiration and are rendered helpless.

But when you give up the painting and return for help, inspiration like a good mother returns and you are once more on your path.

Hold fast to your life, to beauty and happiness and inspiration, and to obedience to inspiration. Do not imitate others or seek advice anywhere except from your own mind. No one can help you. No one knows what your life should be. No one knows what your life or life itself should be because it is in the process of being created.

Life moves according to a growing consciousness of life and is completely unpredictable.

If you live according to human knowledge, according to precept, values, and standards, you live in the past.

If you live entirely in the past you will not know beauty or happiness and you will not in fact live.

You must believe in life. Believe that you can know the truth about life.

You must reject the idea that mankind is in control. That is the same as an ant believing that the anthill is life.

Since we are not in control we need not worry about life, nor about our own lives but wait in readiness.

Suffering in life being a part of life is also positive, since all of life is positive.

Suffering means that you have engaged to resist death and the battle of life and death is on. Life will win.

It was the pull of life that incited you to resist death. That is why I say that the current of the river of life moves us. Awareness of life, beauty, and happiness is the current of the river.

With great awareness we move rapidly. With no awareness we do not move. Life moves on and we remain in death, in confusion and lack of happiness.

I am sure that all of you have had the vision of stepping into a boat and casting off and being afloat on the river of life. That vision is at the urging of life itself.

Those with a strong urge to adventure will move rapidly. Those with security as a goal will not move. Truth is the goal. Truth at whatever the cost — the cost is high in suffering.

Those that want to live a true life, that is a life that is guided by the conscious mind, are surrounded by multitudes that are practically dedicated to ancestor worship.

The multitudes that believe that right and wrong are established and that all that is required is conformity.

The multitudes that give lip service to the transcendent but when the chips are down live a completely materialistic life of conquest and possession.

We don't have to think about the multitudes since all things in life are positive but I assure you that the state of mind necessary to create effective art work is just the opposite of the state of mind of the multitudes.

But we are still not rebels.

To rebel means to destroy existing circumstances. It is anti-life since life is the real creator.

I think you can see that it is life itself that creates life out of death.

 Little Children Loving Love 2001 acrylic and graphite on canvas 60 × 60"

Reflections

I'd like to talk about the perfection underlying life

when the mind is covered over with perfection

and the heart is filled with delight

but I wish not to deny the rest.

In our minds, there is awareness of perfection;

when we look with our eyes we see it,

and how it functions is mysterious to us and unavailable.

When we live our lives it's something like a race — our minds

become concerned and covered over and we get depressed and

have to get away for a holiday.

And then sometimes there are moments of perfection

and in these moments we wonder why we ever thought life was

difficult.

We think that at last our feet are on the right path and that we

will not falter or fail.

We're absolutely convinced we have the solution and then the

moment is over.

Moments of awareness are not complete awareness,

just as moments of blindness are not completely blind.

In moments of blindness when you meet someone you know

well,

they seem hardly recognizable,

and one seems even a stranger to oneself.

These experiences of the mind are too quickly passed over and

forgotten,

although startling moments of awareness are never forgotten.

Seeking awareness of perfection in the mind is called

living the inner life.

It is not necessary for artists to live the inner life.

It is only necessary for them to recognize inspiration or to

represent it.

Our representations of inspiration are far from perfect

for perfection is unobtainable and unattainable.

Moments of awareness of perfection and of inspiration are alike

except that inspirations are often directives to action.

Many people think that if they are attuned to fate, all their

inspirations will lead them toward what they want and need.

But inspiration is really just the guide to the next thing

and may be what we call success or failure.

The bad paintings have to be painted

and to the artist these are more valuable than those paintings

later brought before the public.

A work of art is successful when there is a hint of perfection
present—
at the slightest hint . . . the work is alive.
The life of the work depends upon the observer, according to his
own awareness of perfection and inspiration.
The responsibility of the response to art is not with the artist.
To feel confident and successful is not natural to the artist.
To feel insufficient,
to experience disappointment and defeat in waiting for
inspiration
is the natural state of mind of an artist.
As a result praise to most artists is a little embarrassing.
They cannot take credit for inspiration,
for we can see perfectly, but we cannot do perfectly.
Many artists live socially without disturbance to mind,
but others must live the inner experiences of mind, a solitary
way of living.

  LOVE AND HAPPINESS 2000 acrylic and graphite on canvas 60 × 60"

Beauty is the Mystery of Life

When I think of art I think of beauty. Beauty is the mystery of life.
It is not in the eye it is in the mind. In our minds there is awareness
of perfection.

We respond to beauty with emotion. Beauty speaks a message to us.
We are confused about this message because of distractions. Sometimes we even think that it is in the mail. The message is about
different kinds of happiness and joy. Joy is most successfully represented in Beethoven's ninth Symphony and by the Parthenon.

All art work is about beauty; all positive work represents it and
celebrates it. All negative art protests the lack of beauty in our lives.

When a beautiful rose dies beauty does not die because it is not really
in the rose. Beauty is an awareness in the mind. It is a mental and
emotional response that we make. We respond to life as though it
were perfect. When we go into a forest we do not see the fallen
rotting trees. We are inspired by a multitude of uprising trees. We
even hear a silence when it is not really silent. When we see a newborn baby we say it is beautiful — perfect.

The goal of life is happiness and to respond to life as though it were
perfect is the way to happiness. It is also the way to positive art work.

It is not in the role of an artist to worry about life — to feel responsible for creating a better world. This is a very serious distraction.
All of your conditioning has been directed toward intellectual living.

This is useless in art work. All human knowledge is useless in art work. Concepts, relationships, categories, classifications, deductions are distractions of mind that we wish to hold free for inspiration.

There are two parts of the mind. The outer mind that records facts and the inner mind that says "yes" and "no." When you think of something that you should do the inner mind says "yes" and you feel elated. We call this inspiration.

For an artist this is the only way. There is no help anywhere. He must listen to his own mind.

The way of an artist is an entirely different way. It is a way of surrender. He must surrender to his own mind.

When you look in your mind you find it covered with a lot of rubbishy thoughts. You have to penetrate these and hear what your mind is telling you to do. Such work is original work. All other work made from ideas is not inspired and it is not art work.

Art work is responded to with happy emotions. Work about ideas is responded to with other ideas. There is so much written about art that it is mistaken for an intellectual pursuit.

It is quite commonly thought that the intellect is responsible for everything that is made and done. It is commonly thought that everything that is can be put into words. But there is a wide range of emotional response that we make that cannot be put into words. We are so used to making these emotional responses that we are not consciously aware of them till they are represented in art work.

Our emotional life is really dominant over our intellectual life but we do not realize it.

You must discover the art work that you like and realize the response that you make to it. You must especially know the response that you make to your own work. It is in this way that you discover your direction and the truth about yourself. If you do not discover your response to your own work you miss the reward. You must look at the work and know how it makes you feel.

If you are not an artist you can make discoveries about yourself by knowing your response to work that you like.

Ask yourself: "What kind of happiness do I feel with this music or this picture."

There is happiness that we feel without any material stimulation. We may wake up in the morning feeling happy for no reason. Abstract or nonobjective feelings are a very important part of our lives. Personal emotions and sentimentality are anti–art.

We make art work as something that we have to do not knowing how it will work out. When it is finished we have to see if it is effective. Even if we obey inspiration we cannot expect all the work to be successful. An artist is a person who can recognize failure.

If you were a composer you would not expect everything you played to be a composition. It is the same in the graphic arts. There are many failures.

Art work is the only work in the world that is unmaterialistic. All other work contributes to human welfare and comfort. You can see from this that human welfare and comfort are not the interests of the artist. He is irresponsible because his life goes in a different direction. His mind will be involved with beauty and happiness. It is possible to work at something other than art and maintain this state of mind and be moving ahead as an artist. The unmaterial interest is essential.

The newest trend and the art scene are unnecessary distractions for a serious artist. He will be much more rewarded responding to art of all times and places. Not as art history but considering each piece and its value to him.

You can't think "My life is more important than the work" and get the work. You have to think the work is paramount in your life. An artist's life is adventurous. One new thing after another.

I have been talking directly to artists but it applies to all. Take advantage to the awareness of perfection in your mind. See perfection in everything around you. See if you can discover your true feelings when listening to music. Make happiness your goal. The way to discover the truth about this life is to discover yourself. Say to yourself: "What do I like and what do I want." Find out exactly what you want in life. Ask your mind for inspiration about everything.

Beauty illustrates happiness; the wind in the grass, the glistening waves following each other, the flight of birds, all speak of happiness.

The clear blue sky illustrates a different kind of happiness and soft dark night a different kind. There are an infinite number of different kinds of happiness.

The response is the same for the observer as it is for the artist. The response to art is the real art field.

Composition is an absolute mystery. It is dictated by the mind. The artist searches for certain sounds or lines that are acceptable to the mind and finally an arrangement of them that is acceptable. The acceptable compositions arouse certain feelings of appreciation in the observer. Some compositions appeal to some and some to others.

But if they are not accepted by the artist's mind they will not appeal to anyone. Composition and acceptance by mind are essential to art work. Commercial art is consciously made to appeal to the senses, which is quite different. Art work is very valuable and it is also very scarce. It takes a great deal of application to make a composition that is totally acceptable. Beethoven's Symphonies with every note composed represent a titanic human effort.

To progress in life you must give up the things that you do not like. Give up doing the things that you do not like to do. You must find the things that you do like. The things that are acceptable to your mind.

You can see that you will have to have time to yourself to find out what appeals to your mind. While you go along with others you are not really living your life. To rebel against others is just as futile. You must find your way.

Happiness is being on the beam with life — to feel the pull of life.

  TRANQUILITY 2001 acrylic and graphite on canvas 60 × 60"

The Untroubled Mind

People think that painting is about color

It's mostly composition

It's composition that's the whole thing

The classic image —

Two late Tang dishes, one with a flower image,

one empty — the empty form goes all the way to heaven

It is the classic form — lighter weight

My work is anti-nature

The four-story mountain

You will not think form, space, line, contour

Just a suggestion of nature gives weight

light and heavy

light like a feather

you get light enough and you levitate

When I say it's alive, it's inspired

alive

Inspiration and life are equivalents and they come from

outside

Beauty is pervasive

inspiration is pervasive

We say this rose is beautiful

and when this rose is destroyed then we have lost something

so that beauty has been lost

When the rose is destroyed we grieve

but really beauty is unattached

and a clear mind sees it

The rose represents nature

but it isn't the rose

beauty is unattached, it's inspiration — it's inspiration

The development of sensibility, the response to beauty

In early childhood, when the mind is untroubled, is when

inspiration is most possible

The little child just sitting in the snow

The education of children — social development is contradictory

to aesthetic development

Nature is conquest, possession, eating, sleeping, procreation

It is not aesthetic, not the kind of inspiration I'm interested in

Nature is the wheel

When you get off the wheel you're looking out

You stand with your back to the turmoil

You never rest with nature, it's a hungry thing

Every animal that you meet is hungry

Not that I don't believe in eating

but I just want to make the distinction between

art and eating

This painting I like because you can get in there and rest

The satisfaction of appetite happens to be impossible

The satisfaction of appetite is frustrating

So it's always better to be a little bit hungry

That way you contradict the necessity

Not that I'm for asceticism

but the absolute trick in life is to find rest

If there's life in the composition it stimulates your life moments,

your happy moments, your brain is stimulated

Saint Augustine says that milk doesn't come from the mother

I painted a painting called *Milk River*

Cows don't give milk if they don't have grass and water

Tremendous meaning of that is that painters can't give

anything to the observer

People get what they need from a painting

The painter need not die because of responsibility

When you have inspiration and represent inspiration

The observer makes the painting

The painter has no responsibility to stimulate his needs

It's all an enormous process

No suffering is unnecessary

All of it is only enlightening, this is life

Asceticism is a mistake

sought out suffering is a mistake

but what comes to you free is enlightening

I used to paint mountains here in New Mexico and I thought

my mountains looked like ant hills

I saw the plains driving out of New Mexico and I thought

the plain had it

just the plane

If you draw a diagonal, that's loose at both ends

I don't like circles — too expanding

When I draw horizontals

you see this big plane and you have certain feelings like

you're expanding over the plane

Anything can be painted without representation

I don't believe in influence

unless it's you, yourself following your own track

Why, you'd never get anywhere

I don't believe in the eclectic

I believe in the recurrence

That this is a return to classicism

Classicism is not about people

and this work is not about the world

We called Greek classicism Idealism

Idealism sounds like something you can strive for

They didn't strive for idealism at all

Just follow what Plato has to say

Classicists are people that look out with their back to the world

It represents something that isn't possible in the world

More perfection than is possible in the world

It's as unsubjective as possible

The ideal in America is the natural man

The conqueror, the one that can accumulate

The one who overcomes disadvantages, strength, courage

Whereas inspiration, classical art depends on inspiration

The Sylphides — I depend on the muses

Muses come and help me now

It exists in the mind

Before it's represented on paper it exists in the mind

The point — it doesn't exist in the world

The classic is cool

a classical period

it is cool because it is impersonal

the detached and impersonal

If a person goes walking in the mountains that is not detached

and impersonal, he's just looking back

Being detached and impersonal is related to freedom

That's the answer for inspiration

The untroubled mind

Plato says that all that exists are shadows

To a detached person the complication of the involved life

is like chaos

If you don't like the chaos you're a classicist

If you like it you're a romanticist

Someone said all human emotion is an idea

Painting is not about ideas or personal emotion

When I was painting in New York I was not so clear about that

Now I'm very clear that the object is freedom

not political freedom, which is the echo

not freedom from social mores

freedom from mastery and slavery

freedom from what's dragging you down

freedom from right and wrong

In Genesis Eve ate the apple of knowledge

of good and evil

When you give up the idea of right and wrong

you don't get anything

What you do is get rid of everything

freedom from ideas and responsibility

If you live by inspiration then you do what comes to you

you can't live the moral life, you have to obey destiny

you can't live the inspired life and live the conventions

you can't make promises

The future's a blank page

I pretended I was looking at the blank page

I used to look in my mind for the unwritten page

if my mind was empty enough I could see it

I didn't paint the plane

I just drew this horizontal line

Then I found out about all the other lines

But I realized what I liked was the horizontal line

Then I painted the two rectangles

correct composition

if they're just right

You can't get away from what you have to do

They arrive at an interior balance

like there shouldn't need to be anything added

People see a color that's not there

our responses are stimulated

I'm painting them for direct light

With these rectangles I didn't know at the time exactly why

I painted those rectangles

From Isaiah, about inspiration

"Surely the people is grass"

You go down to the river

you're just like me

an orange leaf is floating

you're just like me

Then I drew all those rectangles

All the people were like those rectangles

they are just like grass

That's the way to freedom

If you can imagine you're a grain of sand

you know the rock ages

If you imagine that you're a rock

rock of ages cleft from me

let me hide myself in thee

You don't have to worry

if you can imagine that you're a rock

all your troubles fall away

It's consolation

Sand is better

You're so much smaller as a grain of sand

We are so much less

These paintings are about freedom from the cares of this world

from wordliness

Not religion

You don't have to be religious to have inspirations

Senility is looking back with nostalgia

senility is lack of inspiration in life

Art restimulates inspirations and awakens sensibilities

that's the function of art

A boy whenever he had a problem

he called this rock up out of the mud

he turned into a rock

he summoned a vision of quiet

The idea is independence and solitude

nothing religious in my retirement

religion from my point of view

it's about this grass

The grass enjoyed it when the wind blew

It really enjoyed the wind leaning this way and that

So the grass thought the wind is a great comfort

besides that it blows the clouds here which make rain

In fact we owe all our self being to the wind

We should tell the wind our gratitude

perhaps if we fall down and abase ourselves

We can get more — we can avoid suffering

That's religion

solitude and independence for a free mind

Nothing that happens in your life makes inspiration

When your eyes are open

you see beauty in anything

Blake's right about there's no difference

between the whole thing

and one thing

Freedom from suffering

suffering is necessary for freedom from suffering

First you have to find out about what you're suffering from

My painting is about impotence

We are ineffectual

In a big picture a blade of grass amounts to not very much

Worries fall off you when you can believe that

pride is in abeyance when you think that

One thing I've got a good grip on is remorse

The whole wave

It applies to life, the wave

As it was in the beginning, there was no division

and no separation

Don't look at the stars

Then your mind goes freely — way, way beyond

Look between the rain

the drops are insular

Try to remember before you were born

The conqueror will fight with you

if there's no one else around

I am constantly tempted to think that I can help save myself

by looking into my mind I can see what's there

by bringing thoughts to the surface of my mind I can watch

them dissolve

I can see my ego and see its intentions

I can see that it is the same as all nature

I can see that it is myself and impotent like all nature

impotent in the process of dissolution of ego, of itself

I can see that its main intention is the conquest and destruction

of ego, of self

and can only go back and forth in constant battle with itself

repeating itself

It would be an endless battle if it were all up to ego

because it does not destroy and is not destroyed by itself

It is like a wave

it makes itself up, it rushes forward getting nowhere really

it crashes, withdraws and makes itself up again

pulls itself together with pride

towers with pride

rushes forward into imaginary conquest

crashes in frustration

withdraws with remorse and repentance

pulls itself together with new resolution

Individually and collectively the same

children trained in pride and patriotism

towering in national spirit

charging in conquest

Victory and defeat and frustration

withdrawing and repentance

then once more pride

the wheel of life

pride

conquest

Victory defeat frustration

remorse repentance

resolution

pride

More people at an earlier age see the conqueror in themselves

then see the way out in another process

the real defeat of ego in which we have no part

The dissolution of ego in reality as it was in the beginning as it was before we were separate and insular

the process we call destiny

in which we are the material to be dissolved

We eat

We procreate

We die

We can see the process and recognize suffering as the defeat of

ego by the process of destiny

We can relinquish pride, conquest, remorse and resolution

inevitably as destiny unfolds

Cradled on the mountain I can rest

Solitude and freedom are the same

under every fallen leaf

Others do not really exist in solitude, I do not exist

no thinking of others even when they are there, no interruption

a mystic and a solitary person are the same

Night, shelterless, wandering

I, like the deer, looked

finding less and less

living is grazing

memory is chewing cud

wandering away from everything

giving up everything

not me anymore, any of it

retired ego, wandering

on the mountain

no more conquests, no longer an enemy to anyone

ego retired, wandering

no longer a friend, master, slave

all the opposites dead to the world and himself unresponsible

perhaps I can now really enjoy sailing

adventure in the dark

very exciting

Beast seems to be stretched out dead

He is very mild

I will not be seeking adventure but it might happen I suppose

Inspired action is destiny

our feet are in the paths of righteousness

the paths that our feet take are marked

As the river runs to the sea

and the plant grows to the sun

so do we flow and grow and exist

Ecstasy playing with Sylphides angels

As long as I look in my mind and see nothing at all

The Sylphides have the beast captured and are grooming him

very pleasant sun, that is what destiny is like

it is like grooming

The idea

the sudden realization of the destruction of innocence by ego

In solitude there is consolation

thinking of others and myself, even plants

I am immediately apprehensive

because my solitude has been interrupted

solitude, inspiration

Westward down the mountain

I am nothing absolutely

There is this other thing going on

the purification of reality

that is all that is happening

all that happens is that process

not nature, the dissolution of nature

The error is in thinking we have

a part to play in the process

As long as we think that, we are in resistance

I can see that I have nothing to do with the process

It is very pleasant

The all of all, reality, mind

the process of destiny

like the ocean full to the brim

like a dignified journey with no trouble and no goal on and on

Solitude

other than nature

smiling

Everyone is chosen and everyone knows it

including animals and plants

There is only the all of the all

everything is that

every infinitesimal thought and action is part and parcel of

a wonderful victory

"freedom on the mountain, a glimpse of victory"

We seem to be winning and losing,

but in reality there is no losing

The wiggle of a worm as important as the assassination of a

president

 TRANQUILITY 2000 acrylic and graphite on canvas 60 × 60"

The Still and Silent in Art

When interest in graphic art wanes I suppose it is possible to imagine its slipping out of sight but I do not believe in that possibility.

My interest is in experience that is wordless and silent, and in the fact that this experience can be expressed for me in art work which is also wordless and silent. It is really wonderful to contemplate the experience and the works. I am sure there will always be some who make this response who will want to try to express it graphically.

But with regard to the inner life of each of us it may be of great significance. If we can perceive ourselves in the work — not the work but ourselves when viewing the work then the work is important. If we can *know our response*, see in ourselves *what we have received* from a work, that is the way to the understanding of truth and all beauty.

We cannot understand the process of life — that is everything that happens to everyone. But we can know the truth by seeing ourselves, by seeing the response to the work in ourselves.

Those who depend upon the intellect are the many. Those who depend upon perception alone are the few.

We perceive — We see. We see with our eyes and we see with our minds. We want to see the truth about life and all of beauty.

Both are a great mystery to us.

Perceiving is the same as *receiving* and it is the same as *responding*. Perception means all of them. It goes on all the time whether we are asleep or awake. When we wake we can recall that which we perceived while sleeping.

Perception is a function. A function is part of a process. It does not identify. We are not identified by perception.

We also think. Perception is the primary experience. Thinking; we consider that which we have perceived. It is a secondary experience. Thinking compares everything that we have perceived with everything that we are perceiving at the moment.

There is no difference between thinking and relative living. Thinking leads to pride, identification, confusion, and fear.

Work is a function in which we seem to be identified. But in reality work is a part of the process of life in which we cannot perceive the beginning or end of our function. We have no understanding of the process of life, in whole, or in part, and we never will. We cannot therefore identify ourselves with our work. Since the process of life reaches to the furthest star the work of each of us is of no significance in the process. In *the great process,* in the sum total of the outward being of all living things our work is insignificant, *infinitesimal and insignificant. This must be realized.*